What's the difference?
Insects

Stephen Savage

HODDER
Wayland

What's the difference?

Amphibians   Insects
Birds   Mammals
Fish   Reptiles

Cover: A swallowtail butterfly and (inset) a seven-spot ladybird.

Title page: Dragonfly larva in its final stage; a green tiger beetle.

Contents page: The caterpillar of a swallowtail butterfly.

Consultant: Carol Levick, Education Unit,
Natural History Museum
Editor: Rosemary Ashley
Series Editors: Katie Orchard & Polly Goodman
Designer: Mark Whitchurch
Paperback cover design: Hodder Wayland

First published in Great Britain in 1999
by Wayland Publishers Limited
This paperback edition published in 2002
by Hodder Wayland, an imprint of Hodder
Children's Books

Hodder Children's Books
A division of Hodder Headline Limited
338 Euston Road, London NW1 3BH

British Library Cataloguing in Publication Data
Savage, Stephen
  Insects. - (What's the difference?)
  1. Insects - Juvenile literature
  I. Title
  595.7

ISBN 0 7502 4153 5

Typeset by Mark Whitchurch, Hove, England
Printed and bound in Hong Kong

Contents

What a difference!

Insect characteristics

- Insects have three parts to their body.
- Most insects have six legs.
- Insects have large compound eyes so that they can see all around.
- Most insects have wings.

There are more insects in the world than any other animal. They all have similar features but their size, colour and shape can be very different.

▼ The largest beetles are male Hercules beetles. With their giant horns, each of these two fighters measure almost 15 centimetres long.

The young of most insects do not look like their parents. They do not have wings and may have extra legs.

▲ There are many beautiful butterflies and moths. This emperor moth, resting on a tree trunk, has false eye spots to confuse predators.

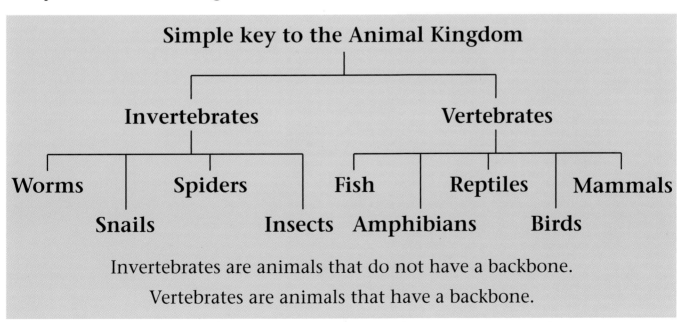

Simple key to the Animal Kingdom

Invertebrates   Vertebrates

Worms   Spiders   Fish   Reptiles   Mammals

Snails   Insects   Amphibians   Birds

Invertebrates are animals that do not have a backbone.
Vertebrates are animals that have a backbone.

Where insects live

Insects are found in many of the world's habitats. They live in forests, grasslands, mountains, deserts, lakes, rivers and ponds. They even live in towns and cities.

Insects have special features that help them cope with the problems of living in these very different places.

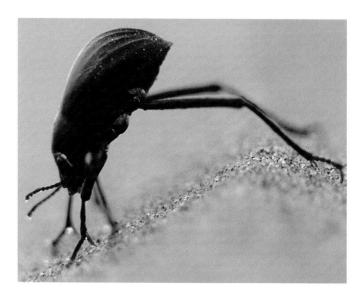

▲ Although the darkling beetle lives in the waterless desert, it obtains water from droplets that form on its body and run down to its mouth.

◄ The morpho butterfly feeds on the juices from overripe fruit in the South American rain forest.

Different habitats

- Insects that live in grass are usually green or brown.
- Pond insects can fly from one pond to another.
- Field crickets lay their eggs underground.
- Desert ants collect and store seeds to eat when there is no other food.

The water boatman lives in ponds. It can breathe underwater because it carries an air bubble beneath its body.

Catching a meal

Some insects eat plants or drink the nectar from flowers. Caterpillars chew the leaves of plants. When they become adult butterflies or moths, most will sip nectar.

Avoiding predators

- Some beetles squirt chemicals at an attacker.
- The caterpillar of a swallowtail butterfly looks like a bird dropping to put off predators.
- Eye spots on a moth or butterfly may frighten off an attacker (see page 5).

▼ Leaf-cutter ants carry leaves back to the nest. The leaves make a garden that grows a special fungus which the ants will eat.

Many insects are predators. They eat other insects and tiny animals which they catch with large, powerful jaws. Huge numbers of army ants on the march can overwhelm insects, small mammals and birds because there are so many of them.

▲ This adult dragonfly waits to catch flying insects with its jaws.

◀ A green tiger beetle feeding on a caterpillar.

Insects are eaten by birds and mammals. To protect themselves, many insects are coloured to help them blend into their surroundings. Some look exactly like sticks, leaves or plants.

The two yellow-and-black striped ▶ hoverflies feeding in the centre of the thistle look like wasps. Most insect-eating animals see the warning colours and keep away.

▼ This praying mantis looks just like a flower. The disguise tricks its prey and also protects it from insect-eating mammals and birds.

▲ A katydid in the South American rain forest mimics a dead leaf so that other insect-eating animals will not recognize it and want to eat it.

Many insects, like wasps, have a sting to protect them, or to paralyze other insects. Some may taste horrible. These type of insects are brightly coloured to warn other animals to stay away.

◄ This close-up picture of a housefly shows its compound eyes, which allow it to see an attacker even from behind.

Hot and cold

Insects are often active on sunny days but find shelter when it is cold. Many flying insects need to warm their wings before they can fly.

How to keep warm and cool

- Some hibernating insects have a chemical in their blood to prevent it from freezing.
- Mountain insects live at temperatures of around 0°centigrade.
- Some moths' bodies are covered in hair to keep them warm.
- Compass termites in Australia build a wedge-shaped nest. The thin edge faces the sun to help keep it cool.

▼ This tortoiseshell butterfly is sunbathing. Many butterflies warm their wings in this way.

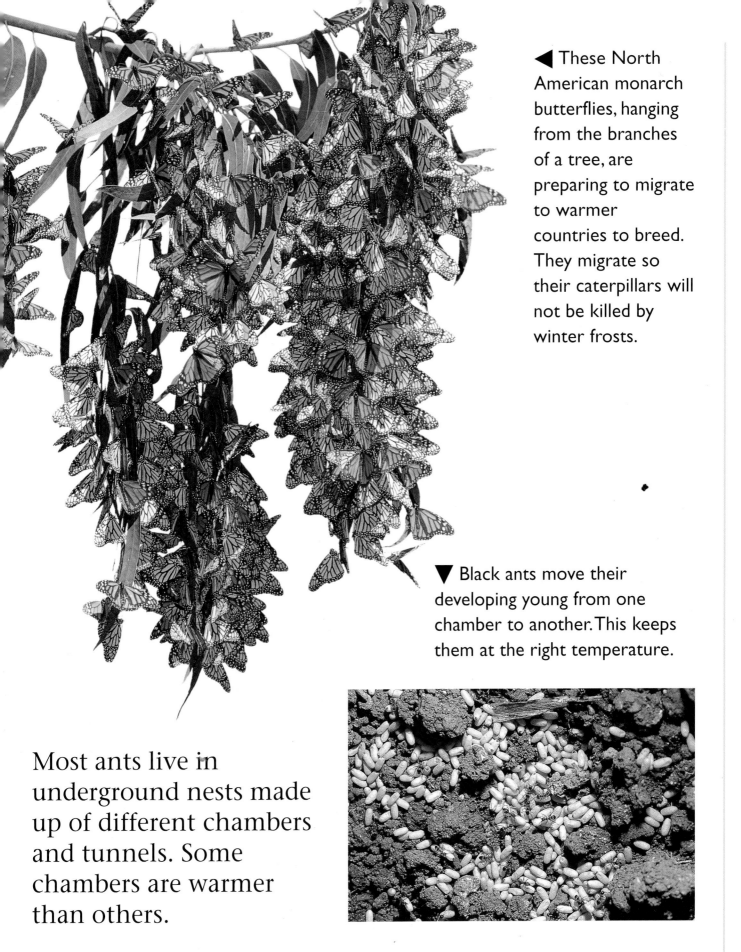

◄ These North American monarch butterflies, hanging from the branches of a tree, are preparing to migrate to warmer countries to breed. They migrate so their caterpillars will not be killed by winter frosts.

▼ Black ants move their developing young from one chamber to another. This keeps them at the right temperature.

Most ants live in underground nests made up of different chambers and tunnels. Some chambers are warmer than others.

On a hot summer's day, ground-living insects stay in the shade. Many desert insects come out only at night, to avoid the blazing sun.

◀ This beetle lives in the Kalahari Desert in Africa. It has long legs so that its body is kept off the scorching sand.

Worker honey ▶ bees at the entrance to the hive. They sometimes fan their wings to help keep the hive cool.

Tiny ant-like termites build special chimneys on the outside of their tall nests. This helps to keep the nest cool.

▼ Termites in Africa build tall nests to allow air to circulate through the chambers. (Inset) Termites inside the nest.

Getting around

Most insects have wings. Butterflies and other flying insects use their wings to fly from place to place, or to escape from danger.

▲ Unlike butterflies that flutter, the hoverfly can hover in the air, or fly off at speed.

Some types of insects walk or run, using their six legs. Their wings are covered by a hard wing case, ready to be opened when they are needed.

Getting around

- Some grasshoppers can leap 70 centimetres.
- Water beetles can swim underwater.
- Some types of insects have two wings and others have four.
- Monarch butterflies fly several thousand kilometres when they migrate to breed.

▲ A stick insect walking up the bark of a tree.

▼ A green tiger beetle can run 60 centimetres a second. This speed is equal to a large mammal running 400 kilometres per hour.

A few types of insect can walk on the surface of still water. They eat other insects that fall onto the surface.

The larvae of many insects are able to move around by wriggling or crawling.

Crickets and ▶ grasshoppers can leap huge distances to escape danger.

▼ Pond skaters have special hairs on their legs that allow them to walk on water.

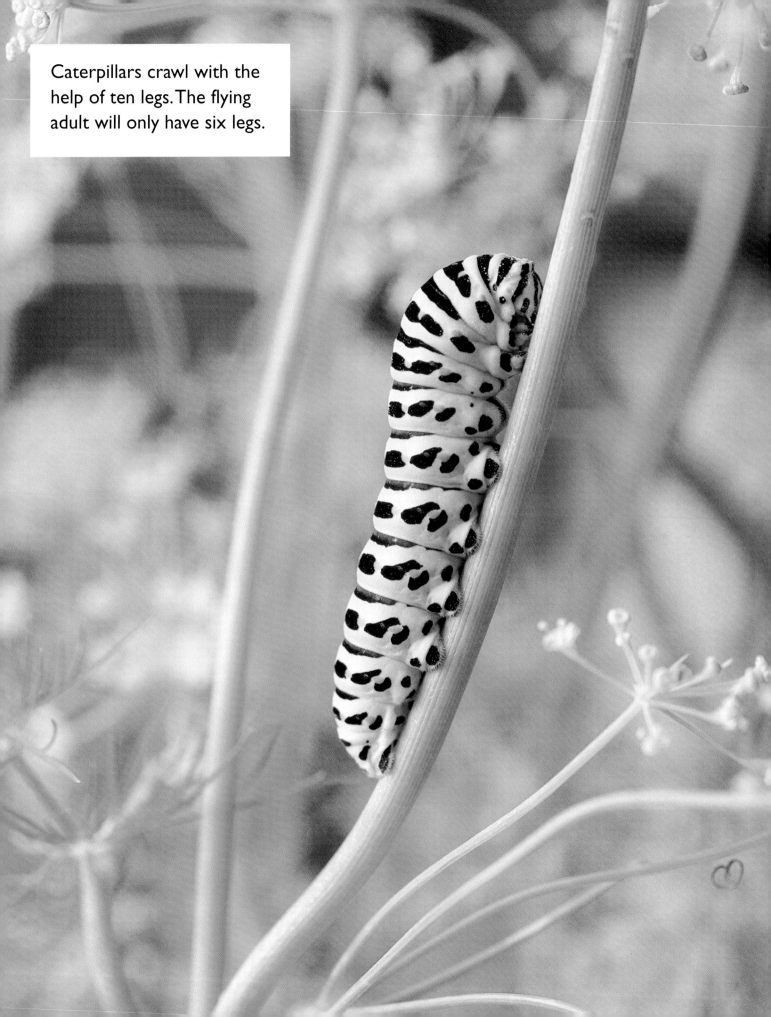

Caterpillars crawl with the help of ten legs. The flying adult will only have six legs.

Insect young

Insects use various ways to attract a mate. Grasshoppers, crickets and a few other insects make sounds. Some female insects produce a scent that attracts a male.

▼ Dragonflies lay their eggs in ponds. The larvae live in the water until ready to become adults. This dragonfly larva is in the final stage before it becomes an adult.

All insects lay eggs. Most types of insect lay hundreds of eggs but only a few will survive to become adults.

Life cycle

- Insects lay eggs.
- Eggs hatch into larvae.
- Larvae become chrysalises (or pupae).
- Adult insects emerge from pupae.

▼ The dung beetle lays an egg on a dung ball that it has made from animal dung. The egg is buried with other dung balls, each in a special chamber.

Some insects take great care of their young. They will even defend them against predators much larger than themselves.

▲ A female shield bug protects her eggs and young with her shield-like body. The young bugs look just like their parents.

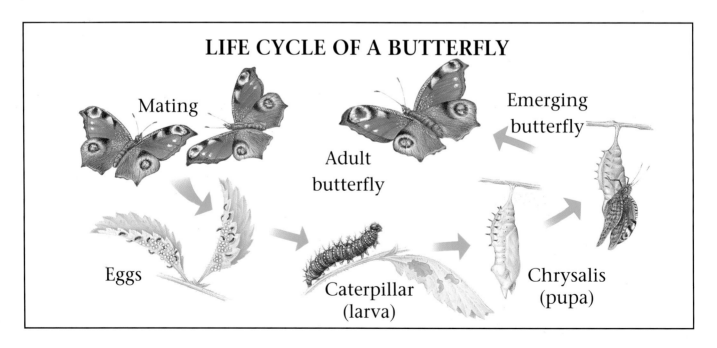

LIFE CYCLE OF A BUTTERFLY

Mating

Adult butterfly

Emerging butterfly

Eggs

Caterpillar (larva)

Chrysalis (pupa)

▼ Honey bee larvae develop within brood cells. They are protected by the rest of the bee colony.

Honey bees and ants live in large colonies ruled by a queen. Most of the colony is made up of workers who collect food and look after the young.

Insect pets

Not many insects make good pets. Your garden is the best place to watch insects, especially around plants and under stones and logs.

◀ Stick insects are sometimes kept as pets.

Looking after insects

- You need a tank with a lid and airholes.
- Provide the right food to eat.
- Give them twigs and foliage for climbing on.
- If you keep insects in a pond tank you will need an air pump.

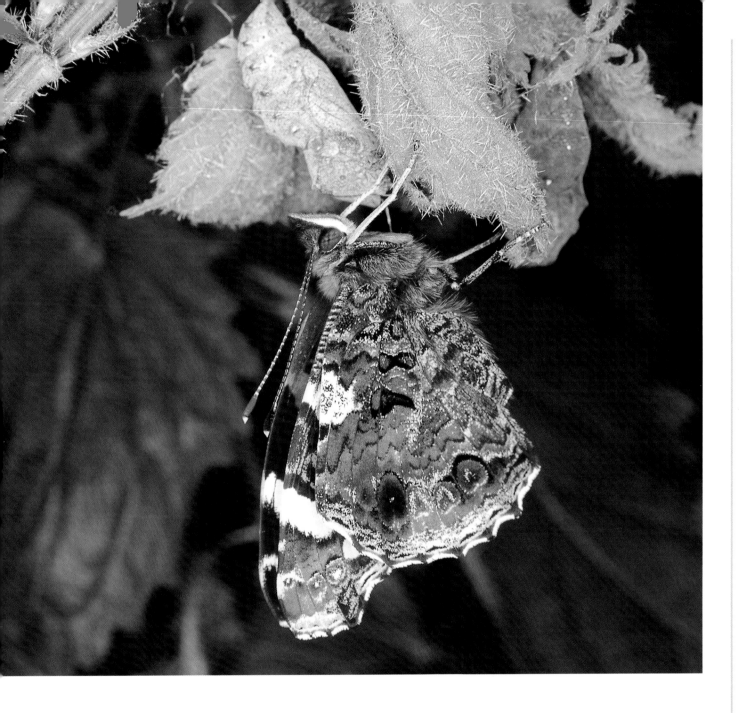

Many insects are attracted to gardens by flowers. They feed on their nectar and pollinate them with pollen from other flowers so they can reproduce. Insects and flowers need each other to survive.

▲ Keep caterpillars in a tank to watch them change, first into chrysalises and then into butterflies. This red admiral butterfly has emerged from its chrysalis.

Unusual insects

A few insects are among the most amazing creatures of the animal world. Some are very brightly coloured or have bodies that are very strangely shaped.

▲ The back end of the hawk moth caterpillar looks like the head of a snake. This frightens away most attackers.

◀ The bodies of some honey pot worker ants become honey stores, to feed the ant community when food is scarce.

The lives of some insects are so unusual that they appear strange even for insects.

▼ Chemicals inside a female glow-worm's body produce a light that attracts male glow-worms.

Parasite insects

- Fleas live on the bodies of larger animals.
- A female mosquito bites animals and humans to obtain blood which helps her eggs develop.
- Greenfly suck the juices from plants.

Scale of insects

Adult Human Hand | Swallowtail Butterfly | Morpho Butterfly | Hercules Beetle | Emperor Moth | Dragonfly | Praying Mantis

Adult Human Finger | Darkling Beetle | Water Boatman | Field Cricket | Army Ant | Leaf-cutter Ant

Adult Human Finger | Black Ant, Worker | Honey Bee, Worker | Desert Beetle | Termite, Worker | Pond Skater

| Leaf Katydid | Tortoiseshell Butterfly | Monarch Butterfly | Stick Insect | Shield Bug | Hawkmoth Caterpillar | Adult Human Hand |

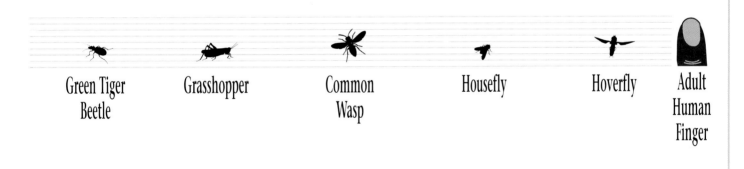

| Green Tiger Beetle | Grasshopper | Common Wasp | Housefly | Hoverfly | Adult Human Finger |

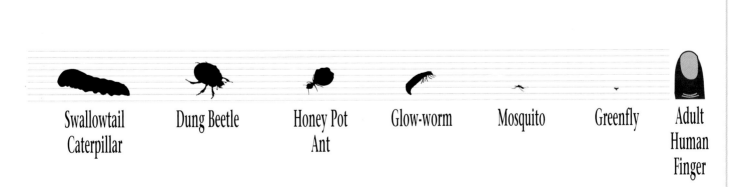

| Swallowtail Caterpillar | Dung Beetle | Honey Pot Ant | Glow-worm | Mosquito | Greenfly | Adult Human Finger |

Topic Web

SCIENCE

Classification.

Life cycles.

How insects adapt to their environment.

Food chains.

Predators and prey.

GEOGRAPHY

Insect habitats - forests, grasslands, deserts, mountains, rivers and ponds.

MATHS

Measure and compare different insects with each other.

ART/CRAFT

Paint a mural showing different insects.

Make a life-cycle mobile.

DRAMA/DANCE

Mime the stages of a caterpillar changing into a butterfly.

Improvise dances to show the ways different types of insects move.

ENGLISH

Write about a day in the life of a chosen insect.

Activities

Science Look for mini creatures in your garden or school grounds. Collect some of them and write down what you find out about them. Check the key on page 5 and decide which are insects (see also 'Characteristics' on page 4). Library books will help you to decide what groups the other mini creatures belong to.

Geography List the habitats in which various insects live. Look up the habitats in an atlas and draw a simple world map showing these habitats and which insects live in them.

Art/Craft Make a mobile showing the life cycle of a butterfly or moth. You can hang the chrysalis, caterpillar and egg at different heights from the adult.

English Write a diary entry describing a day in the life of a worker ant (or any insect of your choice). What does a worker ant do in a day; for instance collect food, care for the ant larvae, prepare the nest.

Drama/Dance Mime the life-cycle of a butterfly – the egg, caterpillar, chrysalis, emerging butterfly and finally the adult, flying away. Create a dance to show how different insects move; flying, crawling, running, leaping, swimming.

Maths Use the scale on pages 28–9 to compare the sizes of different insects with each other. Compare their sizes with the size of your hand or of your index finger. Are any of the insects bigger than your hand?

Glossary

Brood cells The chambers of a bees' nest or hive where the young develop.

Compound eyes The eyes of insects, which are made up of hundreds of tiny lenses.

Habitat The natural home of plants and animals.

Hibernate To spend the winter in a state similar to sleep.

Katydid A type of grasshopper, found in the Americas.

Larvae Grubs or insects after they have left eggs but before they become adults. A single grub is a larva. The larvae of butterflies and moths are called caterpillars.

Migrate To move from one region to another in search of food or a warmer climate.

Nectar A sugary substance produced by plants to attract insects.

Pollinate To fertilize plants and flowers with pollen so that they will produce seeds.

Predators Animals that hunt others for food.

Prey Animals that are hunted and killed for food.

Queen The fertile female amongst a colony of ants, bees or other similar insects.

Finding out more

Books to read

Explorers: Butterflies and Moths by John Feltwell (Dorling Kindersley, 1998)

From Caterpillar to Butterfly by Gerald Legg (Watts, 1997)

My Best Book of Creepy Crawlies by Claire Llewellyn (Kingfisher, 1998)

Wings, Stings and Wriggly Things: Minibeasts by M. Jenkins (Walker, 1996)

Videos

Amazing Animals: Creepy Crawly Animals (Dorling Kindersley, 1999)

Amazing Animals: Minibeasts (Dorling Kindersley, 1996)

Eyewitness: Butterfly and Moth (Dorling Kindersley, 1996)

Eyewitness: Insects (Dorling Kindersley, 1996)

Index

Page numbers in **bold** refer to photographs.

Picture Acknowledgements:

Bruce Coleman Ltd 26(lower), /M.P.L. Fogden 4, /Andrew Purcell 5, /David Hughes 6(top), /Luiz Marigo 6(lower), /Kim Taylor 7, 9(top), /Andrew Purcell 9(lower), /Jenny Grayson 10(top), /Kevin Rushby 10(lower), /Luiz Marigo 11(top), /Kim Taylor 11(lower), /Harold Lange 12, /Ingo Arnot 13(top), /Jeremy Grayson 13(lower), /Kim Taylor 14(top), /Janos Jurka 15, /Kim Taylor 15(inset), 16, /Leonard Lee Rue 17(top), /Andrew Purcell 17(lower) and title page, /J. Brackenbury 18(top), /Kim Taylor 18(lower), Jens Rydell 19 and contents page, /Jane Burton 20 and title page, /Kim Taylor 21, /Frieder Sauder 22, /Kim Taylor 23, /Jane Burton 25, /Peter Evans 26(top), /Peter Hinchcliffe 26(lower); Discovery Books 24(lower); FLPA /B. Borrell cover (inset), /Chris Mattison 14(lower); Oxford Scientific Films /David Dennis; Tony Stone Worldwide /A. Bumgarner cover; Wayland Picture Library 24(top). Artwork on pages 28-9 by Mark Whitchurch and on page 22 by John Yates.